Spilling Kingdoms
-POEMS & PROSE-

Nefisa
WASHINGTON DC

Spilling Kingdoms

Copyright © Y. Misdaq 2011

All rights reserved. This book, or parts thereof, may not be reprinted or distributed in any form without prior permission of the author. However, those wishing to cite, discuss or use this book in any way beneficial to humankind are encouraged to contact the author.

03. Cakes & grapefruit

Published by Nefisa UK
NEFI-BK05
First Edition

ISBN 10: 0-9555024-4-6
ISBN 13: 978-0-9555024-4-6

Printed and bound in America

Foreword

Dare to read aloud —to savour more deeply— this book of poems by the young English/Afghan Yusuf Misdaq, either alone or with someone you love, and you may find yourself forgetting who you are, and where, and without a care in the world. You will have been in an enchanted verbal soundscape of indubitable genius that only real poets can make their own, stranded peacefully, happy to have become lost, and now found.

Recently transported to America and only twenty-six, Yusuf Misdaq already has found his voice and become alert to his gift, with a pen ready for whatever fleeting inspiration tomorrow may bring, wondering if anyone will share the spontaneity and generosity of his own feeling.

I find a new magic in this English, and a critical sensitivity shaped partly by the more traditional culture with which England and America are presently at odds. The author feels no reluctance to bare his love for the Koran, nor any need to apologize for some astutely angular social commentary. He could be, and therefore in a sense already is, "everybody's beloved grandson," rescuing fleeting jewels of delicate nuances from within the frantic rhythms of now, and earning our blessings for an endangered "interiority."

Here is a poet of no little promise. But read him aloud, in your own rhythm, and let your ears tell you what is true. Mind will gladly surrender judgment.

-Ernest G. McClain, Washington, DC, January 27, 2009

Spilling Kingdoms

After Surah al-Fatiha

In the starry space
In the blackness of vacuum and still-silence
Where your soul is not alive.
Among the rounded, shaded orbs which hang like drops of
huge hushedness

There is an invisible wave the size of an invasion fleet of
billions.
It ripples through the blackness and has no sound.

If you were alive to let it pass through you
You, You'd feel kindness flood you.
Gargling love would bubble up from your silly human throat
And salty tears would not run down your
Charming cheeks,
But rise upwards
Above the blackness of space
And into a throne above existence

Where sits a Being.

A BEING BEYOND
3rd July 2008, Elmhurst, Queens, NYC

After Surah al-Qadr

It is waited.
The wait is hung over you like a shawl
Embellished and ornamented
Stylised and refined;
You have no idea.

It is towards your night of power that you slowly go.
With each day the hitherto invisible shawl increases in your sight.

And as years become you
The beauty of your mirror increases.
There is no tiredness or wrinkles as
Your eyes become framed in an Eastern night of
Believing black
Where your two white orbs become a full moon of light
With dark Jupiters inside them
And souls inside the Jupiters.

This is the beautiful face that you see
Thinned and elegant
Which has the look of patience
Proportion and a wild, tender beauty, birthed from
Abstinence.

FOLLOW THE SILENT STONE
(YOU WHO HAVE FAITH)
4th July, Elmhurst, Queens, NYC

For some words we each have our own particular associations. For me, grace & gracious, are very distinct things. They are different to me. Grace is an abstract and wonderful concept, angelic. I am not good at describing it though, and that's because I feel it less. What I find so powerful about Gracious is the image which that word evokes. It is of an Afghan man at an evening house party; the sort that my father attended in London when I was young (various smart, Western suited and educated Afghan men would stand around a nice front room, deep into the night, talking about politics at a time when politics needed to be talked about). This one I see now is a slightly older man, in his 60's perhaps, and somewhat frail. His skin is darker, where most of the Afghans at the gathering, my family especially, are more lighter-skinned. He is thinner than the rest, and has a smile that is so kind. The sort of smile that endears you to someone. Why? Because he seems to go inwards as he smiles, almost as if he is shy and looking away, almost like a beautiful girl, almost like he is wincing, and his eyes are narrowing. Humility seems to have suddenly shined under his face, and whilst he knows so much, he is vulnerable and not confident in himself.

Gracious.

And then I imagine what the <u>most</u> gracious would be like. I marvel at even the supposed 'weaker' personality traits like vulnerability, and humility being magnified to an unimaginable degree. What does humility at its height mean? Just to approach that thought boggles the mind in wonderment.

4th July, Elmhurst, Queens, NYC

On a busy F-Train to Queens

1

This Earth tumbles towards us
                        like a mistake

Like a stumbling woman falling forwards

Spilling white water from crystal glasses into the black air.

2

The people here are very dear to me.
Even the bastards.

5th July, NYC Subway Train to Jackson Heights

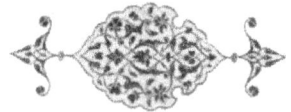

But as soon as he gets up and has a peek, he's back down again, and he sighs to himself in a dejected way, as if he thinks he'll never get off this stinking train.

'Don't worry,' I think to him, 'It will all be over soon.'

Spiders

The sky is not as vast at night
Not as open, and certainly not as trustworthy.
There are no stars, just cloud-cover and the odd firework
Which makes you think that someone in the city is having a good life.

I do not hate the night.

I do not hate spiders, either

And yet I cannot understand them.
And yet they do not please me.
They are living needles
With silent pin-sphere minds
And it's impossible to know just how far their intellect reaches
Even if it is blind and halved
Without emotion or radiance.

> As a working insomniac
> The night has been my friend.
> Only now I wonder if that is because I knew it would end.

The night does not hate me.
Spiders do not hate you.
But are they not *evil*?
Are they not?

Do they not move with calculations

And deadly intent?
Do they not weave spells for death
And paralysis?

They are not vegetarian, and even if they were
I would free a leaf if I saw it caught up in that no-world
That waiting for death in the wind-world
The nightmare silk route.

I try to think of taking refuge in the fact of their
Small size
Of my physical advantage over them.

But this is no good.

They are symbols.
And if symbols of the mind can dominate
Like a nightmare of a man you love
Suddenly drained of all his humanity
Walking around like a fleshy meat-figure

Then real creatures of Earth, no matter how small
Will dominate too.

And spiders, if you let them, will run you down.

5th July, Elmhurst, Queens, NYC

Like, Totally!
After Surah al-Kawthar

Time spreads across the land; a running sun
Revealing itself over miles of open grass.

Wind lifts you off the ground when you believe in dreams.

Space measures itself silently and can't be expected to prove itself to us.

(God rules)

8th July, Elmhurst, Queens, NYC

Roots (What You Are Made Of)

When I was born
With the movement of water running through me
God promised me victory
If and only if
I would never turn my back on the sea.
Never lift my heart out of the water.

8th July, Central Park, NYC

IF (WINGS ETC.)
For Hamza Yusuf Hanson

If only we would awaken with the morning light
And begin to sing each time
A tuneless, star-filled melody of space.

If and when we could
We would fly from giant tree to giant tree
Following our friends
Thinking of and remembering and wishing for
Music. And more music.

If we flew out of our doors
After breakfast
Into the promising sky
-Unheld by hinge-
-Freedom'd in the bathing air-

If and where we found the air
That gifted confidence in our (speaking) instincts
We might spend the day there, breathing in together
And happiness would follow
And we would return home in the evening

Satiated

Older and better lived.

8th July, Central Park, NYC

For Heaven Her

There, a star for her.

A Star for her crepuscule mind:
A Sierra Leone beach in silence with
Receding waves

And there, a Star embedded in the sand for her
At midnight when the full moon makes
Mansions of the beaches

Connected mansions of on and on

There, the secure and warm weather of night for her
With no wind

To hold her in place and safe
Safe as a blanket around her
Safe as a hedgehog

Now walk, my love
Walk the lawnshores with God.

19th August, Wyoming Avenue, Washington DC

Reed

It's funny,

I read Rumi or Hafez and other Sufi poets, and they can't stop going on about the flute or the reed, and what a metaphor their sound is for the Divine, Life, or something or other... I love flutes. I love the idea of them. Of sound coming from the flow of air from my body. I love the wooden / organic timbre of their sounds too, some of them anyway- the Indian flute and in particular the more earthy Shakuhachi of Japan. I don't like the way Hollywood uses the Western flute (which I think is made of metal). I bought one recently, with the hope of learning it. I liked the idea of learning it. It's not a flute though; I didn't have the money for a flute. It says on the pack, 'Practice Chanter'.

The only noise it makes is a groaning, dying noise. And I keep running out of breath. It changes randomly from a horrible low pitch to a horrible high-pitch, even if I keep my fingering regular, it seems to produce completely different notes each and every single time I blow into it. Blowing into it is no picnic either; I feel like I'm blowing up a balloon, and I've always hated having to blow up balloons, especially in the presence of beautiful women, where the weakness of my lungs would be ruthlessly exposed in a farting flutter of humiliation.

Then again, my fingers used to hurt tremendously when I first started teaching myself guitar. Now the joy of playing something on it far outweighs the almost imperceptible feeling of discomfort (i.e. hard steel strings pressing against my soft fingertips). Maybe one day I will know what it's like to blow into a warm wooden flute and produce something beautiful, something pure and un-pretentious. Then I might read Rumi in Farsi and really feel it.

11th July, McLean, Virginia

Inspired from a glance at an open Qur'an page, 26:43

Amongst you there are those who need action
Those who need psychology
Science, or emotion.

Each of you have different ways of
Circumnavigating a balloon of intrigue
Sizing it up
Predicting precisely what is happening inside

And if necessary, what it symbolizes.

I am another one amongst you.

12th July, McLean, Virginia

Anyone born and shined in the diamond world
Will see the signs of God.

December 2005, Venezia

Yearning to be the most moonshine I can be
See the angel jogging backwards in front of me

"You can do it! You are Jesus Christ!
Iced out with sun, for your life, <u>be someone</u>."

December 2005, Firenze

Fluttering acceleration of birds to
Flickering candle existence.

December 2005, Venezia

When God made the world
He made women first

- I'm not saying anything new here am I? -

Women
Or as I like to call them

Shy-na

Are streamlined and smell
 Wonderful!

There's no stopping them now!

We, on the other hand
Are made as an after-thought.

We are obtuse
Sweaty invaders

God help us.

3rd November 2008, McLean Virginia

This life is so strange.
I cannot sit anywhere without a new noise occurring.
Or a sensation arising. No matter how small.

It would be nice to be able to hold my breath, and have
Everything be suddenly still.
Instead though, I feel pressure on my chest, and the
Need to be released from torture by breathing out.

It would be nice to be able to have zero thought, and zero touch, and zero sound, if only for a few seconds.

But there is nothing you can do about this life.
You cannot end it

And even if you tried
The ring of suicide
Would echo out around your bullet-head
For God knows how long.

The birds, cars, crickets and skies will always
     ring roam tick   and move

The sea will always roar like a silent or screaming Lioness.

Whether you are there before her or not.

And inside your heart there will always be

Scenes

playing out

Your deepest fears, theatre'd
Your desires and dreams, Hollywooded and enshrined in
Pure American Hope.

And in your despair, in your thuds of despair

There will be the silence of a God who knows.

July 12th McLean, Virginia

What Time does with Meaning

Time, by its extinguishing / diminishing nature, should grow its own beard. This should be a Universal beard, for any and all inhabitants of Earth to see, to recognize in their own ways, to confirm in them the aged nature of this old man of a life. This exhausted, disabled life, where even love is distinguished not by its ecstatic fruit, but rather the longing and pain associated with it.

The sad beard of time can be almost anything to anyone. A lesser poet would begin to list each of its possible incarnations at this juncture, impressing you with a list of well thought-out metaphors ('Time's beard is a decaying city street' etc.) Whilst that example makes it abundantly clear that I am not a very good poet myself, my intention is not to dazzle and impress you with lists of well thought-out metaphors. No…

I am interested in the old seed, the colonel kernel, the know-no tree, the unclickable link which is stamped (from the inside) on all of our hearts and betroths us to our ancient culture. Our golden age of spirit. Our heritage-jewels. The God inside.

The inevitable bride.

A young, un-glorious, sweating man who seeks the glorious things, am I. And presently, to my detriment perhaps, I find the act of recognizing / acknowledging this life as a choking, sapping process to be one of the pre-requisites for getting to know its architect, the most kind creator. I think, however, that the time is nearing that this endless theatre of varying colors of SADNESS will soon metamorphose into an endless theatre of LAUGHTER.

Whereupon I shall thereafter become known /
re-incarnated as 'The Laughter Man'. And the beard of time shall become the dance of now.

July 15th 2008, Adams Morgan, Washington DC

Flux

Bleed out your beyond borders
Sleep off the distrusting trees which don't sway to a rhythm.

Ride off with your love on a horse made of
Golden future
Where hope elopes.

Sign your name silently in prayer and
Keep an eye on the antsy soldiers
Pushing for recognition or war.

.Ants in your pants.

Sway to a flexible rhythm
Like wind.

Renounce the known names and shapes of star-clusters.
Think of stars as abstract dots
You will never be able to grid.
Remember you're not seeing them all when you look up.

Let the wild stars spill prologue across your page of plans.

July 21st, McLean, Virginia

1

<u>Proving</u> a heart to be a Good Heart is hard.
Only a Soft-Heart could achieve this
By ignoring the task, serenely.

2

I put my arms
Electric

Out by my side like
Crucifix

The wind will wash my
Wounds

And weave my holey
Spirit.

3

There is God in the tickle
The small hair of nipple

The goose-bumps
Which I must inspect.

And the Royal Spine
Which I Yoga-stretch

4

Wisdom is the wave go'bye
Wisdom is the peach

My old soul is a six and twenty
Unattended on the shimmering beach

5

He is a wave to reach my toes of He
The One is a morning with a
Sun-smile
Yawning.

29th July, McLean, Virginia

If Ali were a color, he would be GOLDEN.
If Abu Bakr were a liquid, he would be tears.
If Umar were a fighter, he'd be a Lover.
If Uthman were alive today,
> he would be ignored by most.

5th August, McLean, Virginia

New place

Do you know the way some organs tremble with each note? I am a musician, I should know the name for this effect. I think it is *tremolo*.

Do you know the jittery, shaking, shrill beauty in the voice of the Portishead lead-singer? I am a musician, I should know her name. I think it is Beth Orton. No, it is Beth *Gibbons*.

Anyway

At times, I were that way too

I'd shimmer and shake and feel so ill at ease
Wonder why I don't pray more
When I know that's the answer

I'd feel like neither sitting nor standing
And my heart
Silent as a stone
Felt as though someone were tearing it away from home
Or bringing it to a new place
And I'd not know what to choose over the

Sitting
        and the
                gaping

It would usually last only a day and a sleepless night. Eventually the automated, rigid

Tremolo effect would be turned off
And I'd walk the new street in some
Major scale of comfort and familiarity.

13th August, 2nd Avenue NYC

bellumber, po-lis, freene, kind of cut off, sincer'd. pu langled. defindris, ridicule scintillator.

It's curious, when the body is empty of energy. I have just enough energy to sit here and stare blankly, thinking of nothing. That's about it. Wolf Blitzer's eager and unintelligent face beams out at me.

He is like a squirrel.

Listen

This world's a flaming joke.

By the time your life is over
It will either make you laugh ceaselessly

Or smoke away to bye-bye
    Ashes to ashes

13th August, 2nd Avenue NYC

Para Keith Olbermann, y el otro Hombres Indignado / Television-Lefties in the last year of Bush the lesser

PIE !

Oh what the hell !

Forget it all !

Forget the tattooed leftists with their hearts all worn out.

Forget the causes which they espouse and push hard like
False pregnancy with no real baby-heart inside.

Who's got time?
Who has the time?

But *right* must be done, they say, we must do *right*!
For our children's sake! they say.

Here's a newsflash for you, pea-brains:

Your children are already smarter than you.

Do you think they would waste their breath
Cynically cutting each other down night after night

When they could be out playing day after day?

I'm serious.

So stuff that wagging flapping tongue of yours down the
front of your pants and tie your belt up <u>tightly</u>!

Or better yet, wear suspenders, like Larry King.

Life's too short to not let looser.

Sit back and relax now
In a chair with an unbuttoned trousers.
Unbuttoned *pants*!
Sit back with a table before you that holds PIE
Nothing but perfect, sweet, PIE.

Stuff your face 'til your heart's content and
Forget all about Bill O'Reilley.

Everything's all right.

                11th September, McLean, Virginia

Englishman in America

There's a group in DC who meet, and call themselves
Green Muslims

I'm on their list and they send me e-vites
Every month or so
Pot luck dinners and so on
'Green topics' to think about and then discuss at the meets
And so on

I'd like to attend, but I just find the whole thing
Preposterous

So I'm a preposterous loner.

I went to perform at another Islamic event in DC once
It was called a dessert party
Only sweets and cakes allowed
And soft drinks
"*Soda!*"

Lots of Pakistani-Americans and lots of sugar

I was upset because I was hungry
But couldn't find anything to eat.

Everyone called me an *Afghani*
And marveled at my British accent.

I ended up hiding in the toilet
Talking to myself in the
Cubicle.

But Americans, they are such a funny people

They mean so well
Organize and categorize so well
Are so very earnest and corny
And yet you can't be so cynical as to mock them
Because
They've got the right idea.
And in your heart, you know they do.

I click the link and fill in the e-vite
Whenever it comes to my inbox
I tick
'Maybe,' I'll attend.

But I never do.

It must be nice though
To belong somewhere.

Late August, McLean, Virginia

Here it's like there
But more hearts and harvests

Here too, grey squirrels
Only more

And because more
Greater awareness of the subtle differences
Greater understanding of the true nature of squirrels

Here it's like there
At more height
With more horror

Here too –though I came to escape it–
Dried up shells of sarcasm also
Play at being human
Succeeding only in moving in
Media-acceptable ways

Proving that this globalized world is
Round

Spilling and slipping across itself.

ENGLISHMAN IN AMERICA # 2
9th November, Farragut Square, Washington DC

INVISIBLE PROGENY GHOSTING ME INSIDE PRETENTIOUSLY-NAMED TEA-HOUSE

Outside of the window, I see the flag of the Embassy of Chad, blowing in the wind. And below it, stuck into the soil, there is a banner. It reads,   OBAMA
                BIDEN

And perhaps or perhaps not, my grandchildren, you will come to know those names quite well.

I am writing at a time when pregnancy resides and things are not settled.

What will you know?

Chirpy little bird-babies.

Whatever will you know?

October, Dupont Circle, Washington DC

What's the sense of it all?
What's the shiver reality?

What's the canonized recital
The Copernican credulity
The siren buffer
The tangled stone
The walking home
The black glasses
The salty pepper
The fertile doctor
The tongue and tongue
The Universes

October, Washington DC

Hadji Murat by Leo Tolstoy

" 'Lya illyakha il Allah."

Oh for a simple life
Of mortal Enemies
Of loyal Friends

Of an immoral world
Which I would Hero and Gentleman.

I wish for the life of a martyr

So that when my head is severed
I shall go to heaven

So that this nuanced, twisting grey life can
Stop dangling around
Year after year
Like some unwanted friend
Attaching himself to me
And never leaving me alone.

Me and my sad face.

28th August, McLean, Virginia

Delegates–Cavaliers–Samurai
Tribesmen–Womenfolk
Workers & Volunteers

Charge!

Puncture this soft world with bayonets and
With bare hands
Rip it apart

Let the only thing standing be gas.

28th August, McLean, Virginia

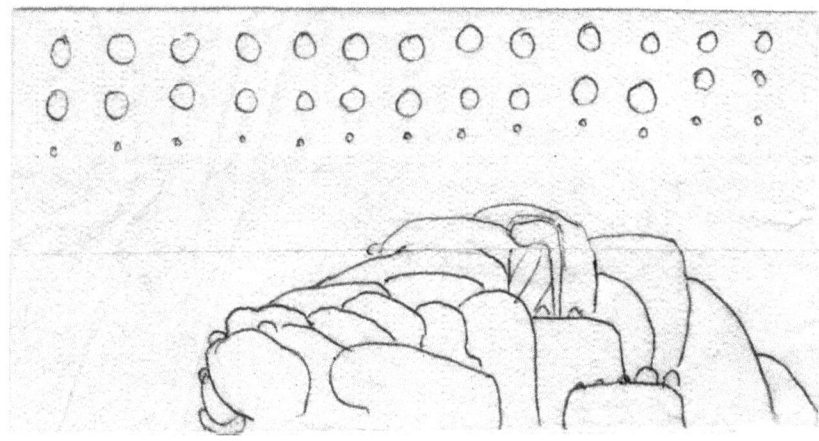

Life and Heaven

There is no limit to the amount of take-offs
Once the Master has you
He will take you from stomach to soil in a 68-year
Flashdream

And you may remember best
A night you lay down your back to grass
With wincing stars on your lashes

And felt no future
Nor remembered no past

And, waking, you may say,
"Here I am.
          Thank you God that I am here."

30th August, McLean, Virginia

During the day
Night stars are flattened
Rolled across the sky like dough

The rolling tickles them
They turn blue with pleasure
And there is your day.

In the night, they focus back in again
Squint, blink and concentrate.

The night clarifies.

DAYS ARE FOR DREAMING
31st August, McLean, Virginia

Listening to God more easily outside the window

Don't be a stranger to me.
Don't forget about me.
Don't love someone else more than you love me.
Don't hurt me.

I said these things silently to the humans I loved because I saw God in them. I didn't know that at the time. I've since understood I was talking only to God, yearning only to Him, and that the people were mere conduits, conductors of the electrical current. When the humans paid no attention to the desires of my heart, and inadvertently hurt me, I re-realized the fact that if God is in everything, then everyone has their own competing claims, and these will sometimes 'clash.' You can't always get what you want... Either we only have a certain, limited portion of God within us, or our muscles & blood cloud out our full divine aspect. I'm inclined to believe the latter. Generally speaking, I often believe the latter. Perhaps that's because it's the latter... Either way, the knowledge that God is within us all must be tempered by an awareness of the real distinction between 'within' and 'omnipresent'. The God that is omnipresent (all around us, abound in the world, roaming) is sometimes easier to pay heed to than the God within, even if they are the very same. We are the problem. In us, the divine is fused with the self, and so given the self's moody nature, we don't quite know who to believe when we look inside. We don't know who's who.

Stepping out of the house, breathing in the majestic wind, the kind wind, seeing greenery, even in small doses, and watching a neighbor in their front garden, involved in some menial, wonderful task, as they call out to an invisible loved one inside the house, having a silly conversation about something practical, like,

"Which brush?"
"The one with the blue handle."
"Oh yes, that one... I don't know."

In such sweeps of outer reality, which can fill the heart with laughter, one feels the presence of a knowing, playful, and ironic God. Ironic to the point of reality. And one may say, "Alhamdullilah[1]," and feel very grateful indeed to be alive, at this time, at your age, in this wonderful place where you live.

September 1st / Ramadhan 1, McLean, Virginia

---

[1] Literally *Praise be to God*; but more wondrous in Arabic, filled with more awe / life than the somewhat over-used phrase suggests to Western ears.

In a warm dawn
On a huge carpet in a forest
Outside a house
Praises are breathed off into the air.
The hanging, honeyed air.

American air.

And the distant neverending rumble of the almighty highway
Miles away
Bounces back to us as
Bass-Whispers from the
Trusted trees.

Ramadawn 5, McLean, Virginia

Even Without Toys (Fasting)

An emptied room, lit from
White light.

A cloudy but bright day.

A slow passing room.

The joy that builds in it during the course of the day
Is invisible
The sober contentedness cannot be explained.
The room is still empty.

And in the evening
The few colorful toys which are scattered on the floor
Make little difference.
They do not explain away the fulfillment.

It is a distant fulfillment
Which we feel only as a daydream
Remembered in fragments.

We know simply that the life
Is good. Even without toys.

Ramadhan 10, McLean, Virginia

Wa ad-Duha, Wa Laylee Itha Sajaa

1

When one has slept
And awoken for dawning
Where mountains tremble at the back / tip of your
Quivering sajjda head

The stillness of last night becomes a distant yet
Related memory to the stillness of this
Dawn.

2

Soft yellow lights and walls
Keep you guessing at the face of the stars
Like Muhammad
An unknown beauty.

3

I go forth
To breathe in the special air of clarity.

Before returning to my in-box
I take in more
Air billowing through me.

Ramadawn 11, McLean, Virginia

There is a black planet
Rolling, stationary.

Spots of neptune-blue blood are seen in the wounds of
The skin of it.

It is silhouetted on the top half by the shimmering
Rays of a white sun
Which is relishing its opportunity
And hoping profusely.

Ramadhan 12, McLean, Virginia

When performed properly
The prayer makes of the standing believer
An unbreakable structure of steel
With crossed arms interlocking.

When rising up from prostration
The head is a searching moon
Mediated on shoulder mountains
And all powerful.

When in prostration
The sadness convulses out
From clasped eyes wincing.
From the remembering heart.

Away into the Air
Ramadhan 12, McLean, Virginia

Pearl

I am waiting to find my place here.
There are all kinds of rushing yellow dots that
Stream past me
Each of them with their own care
Their own hearts protected.

I've given up grabbing at them
Or pretending to look wounded so that they'll
Gravitate towards me through a mercy
Which ticks with an inbuilt countdown.

I want one of them to stop of its own free will
And shoot itself directly into me

I'm unprotected

Ramadawn 15, McLean, Virginia

WAKE UP A NEW MAN

My ! Empty out
Viruses

Hang an empty glass vase
Upside down

Let the nothingness
.Go.

And let go –away– the days
Evil 'n pain, which is symbolic
In your mind and
Nothing at all

Ramadhan 16, Wyoming Ave, Washington DC

Relinquish your rights to property
Ownership of hearts and
Lawn mowers.

You've not been made to cash in
Claim refunds or rebates.

You've been made to empty out your slop buckets
And gush off the waterworks,
Liquids, pipes, pressure and valves.

You've been made to totally fall apart

THE BUILDING (UP)

Ramadhan 22, McLean, VA

The Smell of Rum

I walked down Connecticut Avenue in Washington DC. I had just returned from work, and wanted to walk a little bit more in the beautiful Autumn weather before I got on the Metro (DC's underground system, which features carpeted, leather-seated trains so impeccably clean that you sometimes wonder if you are dreaming when you ride on them). On the likewise spotless streets of North-West DC you will see the very specific class of young American men and women in suits, who have come from some other part of the country and now work in some government or government-related job, in an institute, or a think-tank, or embassy. I suppose I'm one of them now too. You'll see taxis crossing the wide roads at a somber, sleepy pace. There will also be a homeless African-American man, rattling a polystyrene cup with change in it. He will be staring off into space and his rattling of the cup will have a hypnotic effect.

I come to a large crossing. Unlike back home, I cannot be cool and walk straight across it whilst the sign is red. Being a stranger living in a new country makes you more humble, paying more heed to the laws. You feel a little like Winston Smith from Nineteen Eighty-Four, after he has been brainwashed into loving Big Brother. So I wait for the signal and then, as I begin crossing, a short little man hobbles forwards in my direction. It is Donald Rumsfeld.

I go through the usual stages when you realize you are face to face with someone famous. Famous? 'Hi! I love your work! I thought you were great in Abu Ghraib!' No, famous seems a horrifically unusual word to use with such a man. A man I had become so used to perceiving as the powerful face of the American Empire. For a shade of a split second, I think to myself, 'It can't be him,' but then, the evidence is too strong as I look him in the eye. He has no security personnel, it is just the man, just the proposition. As he limps past me on the road, I say, in a daze, almost mechanically and almost like an American, "You son of a bitch!" He does not hear me, and I'm glad. Not because I fear him turning around, and suddenly unfurling bat-like demonic wings, his eyes turning red, him impaling me with his arm (which has morphed into a sharp spike). Not at all. But because I was ashamed of my rudeness. And because I said those words without my heart in them, almost unconsciously. I said them out of a strange duty to the past. Back when I really did see him as some sort of a devil.

That old, meagre man was no devil. His narrow eyes were squinting under his glasses in the sort of desperate way that a scared old mans sometimes will when trying to cross a very large, busy city street all on his own. He looked so fearful. If it were London, or even New York, he would have received a million insults from public-passers by, I'm sure of this. In DC, where everyone plays by the (same) rules, I'm much less sure. The fear I saw in him was not cinematic, dramatic or even incredibly obvious. It was slightly below the surface. Embedded. It is hard to put into words just how much smaller he looked in person. The word 'frail' is the best I can offer. Rummie's lip was quivering as he walked, as he trembled, and to top it all off, he was wearing a blue medical sling on one of his arms. A sling!

And… He didn't matter anymore.

Just like that, he had become 'irrelevant.'

Symbolic.

History.

Tea-House Conversations of DC

In DC, people find themselves using the word <u>savvy</u> a lot.
It just seems to pop up more often here.
Like hummingbirds pop up in Southern California.

The competent man and pretty woman sitting at the small table are still young-ish and *reasonably* attractive.

But instead of badly disguised flirting, they seem to be stuck in one mode. And they totally *love* this mode!

He's talking a lot and telling her about his <u>pro-bono</u> work.
She says to him,
"The work I'm doing now is totally…..Uh.."
He knows where she's going already of course,
And confidently throws in, "Ad-hoc"
"Totally ad-hoc!" She says, unpausing herself and
Fluttering onwards enthusiastically.

And now he is talking about <u>skillsets</u> and
Policy-planning and
THE LEGISLATIVE ARM OF GOVERNMENT!

And she keeps nodding as if it's the English language!

And I wonder

What planet I have arrived on.

18th November, 2008

In the Bag

The white middle-aged man was an expert who worked for someone like Brookings or some other tank of thought. His particular field of expertise was my country, Afghanistan. He knew more facts about it than I do. The corner of his mind that was reserved for Afghan expertise was a sharpened pencil and he continually fed it by staying informed, reading statistics, newspaper reports, giving the occasional interview etc. That corner of his mind provided him with a career. He was a seasoned Washingtonian expert though, so as soon as Afghanistan stopped being fashionable and the funding and media went away from it, he would surely find himself something else to become an expert in.

One day he was sitting in his house, mostly fairly modern ikea furniture with various policy-related books that would not date well on his coffee table. Incidentally, there were also some art and photography coffee-table books. Those were made especially for coffee tables. Nobody was there, but he was talking anyway, in his nasal voice, as if he were conversing with someone, he said something like this,

"Well, see, the laws for lobbying have changed since then…"

As he continued to speak, several thick-set removal men of Latin origin, dressed in removal clothes and holding yellow rags, entered the apartment and began lifting things up and removing them. The apartment emptied, one piece of tidy furniture at a time, although the PhD'd man continued to speak with contained passion about the critical need for the

US Military to remain in Afghanistan.

Two removal men came back for one last thing; they lifted the little man from his backside as though he were a chest of drawers and hauled him outside to the removal truck.

He did not mind.

They placed him neatly into a corner between a fern and a book shelf.

"The only other potential sticking points are Venezuela, Iraq, Pakistan, Iran, Russia and China. Maybe Brazil too."

The removal men gave him a few more shoves to make sure he was tightly snug between the various furnishings and then they walked out, lowering the slide door and leaving him in a darkness which he found acceptable.

Fitra versus Finance

Born Believer

No bandage or blemishes
From before
                When baby

No bollocks or bull   nor
Bland conversation

But

As the bile-years up
Folding and falling and
Bystanding..:

No Butterflies.

Ramadhan 26, West 42nd Street, NYC

Why do I keep turning over like a snake in a swimming pool?

Why am I squirming like a child trying to extricate himself from a vicious parents grip (prelude to a beating)?

Why am I turning my head away sharply at everything that comes my way?

Why do I allow nothing to get into my protected neck, which is
            most sensitive of all?

Why do I wince?

Why always on the verge?

What scared of?

Ramadhan 26, West 42nd Street, NYC

God walketh me across a horizon
Hill shaped.
God pulleth me along t'ward the rolling sunset.
He maketh me to lie down in pastures green at
Summit determined.

There I accept the coming of night

Relent

Drop relinquishing hand

Dangling there
Retired & Reconciled.

Life alone without another kiss.
Life alone under clean
Sparkling Japanese Stars.

Life enough for God to place flowers between my pages
And
    Let them dry between my pressed bookheart.
To render them still and radiating
In the e'er glowing eyes of a history perceiv'd by youth.

Ramadhan 26, West 42nd Street, NYC

Stereotypical DC-Men are not Stereotypical

Today, I ran out of underwear, so I am wearing long johns instead. I am warm.

Some people are so neat and sensical! It's great.
Look at this tidy specimen before me:
He is probably lunching here because of the sudden rain,
Like me.
But he is dressed for the rain. Impeccably.
He has an umbrella, gloves, a light-rain coat
And it hasn't rained in ages. Just today.
He must have a space in his closet for clothes appropriate for
Sudden rainfall.

When he finishes his lunch, he stands up, facing the rain outside, and wastes not a single move. Everything he does is in logical order, economical. He takes out his gloves, lays them out tidily on the table, then he gives his small black umbrella (matching his stylish black coat) a few firm, functional taps to remove any remaining rain, before laying that out onto the table too, alongside the gloves. Then he picks up his finished food and walks to the bin (*trash!*) leaving his accessories alone on the table. He doesn't feel weird leaving them unattended, he knows he is coming back for them, that this is North-West DC, where nobody steals. If it were me, I would have tried to carry everything else with me to the bin, all in one go. I would have dropped things and been untidy about it, and then when I'd have got to the bin, I'd have realized that there was no need to bring everything with me in one go. And even then, I would probably still have forgotten something at the table and had to have returned again anyway, by which point I'd feel as if the eyes of every single person in the small cafe were fixed upon me; and then heat from behind my face would begin to make itself known to me.

This excellent and efficient human being is not dorky or nerdy, if you are imagining such. He is just exceptionally tidy, with perfect hair, and impressively methodical. He's not a stereotype, even though he is. He is a perfectly normal, acceptable member of humanity. And perhaps I am too. The only difference is that he probably does not have a mini-crisis every morning when he can't find his keys before leaving the house. He probably has a drawer specifically for socks which does not get mixed up after a week or so like mine. He is almost certainly not wearing odd socks, as I am now. He is definitely *not* wearing long johns in lieu of underwear.

He and I both exist. And we both have things to offer mankind.

There are wild buffalo's, and there are house-trained felines. And sometimes life will ask him to become a wild buffalo, and other times it will ask me to be a house-trained cat.

There's something exciting about that.

Train Commute to Dupont Circle

I just left West Falls Church station and already I've taken my journal out! Without knowing what to write! What am I nuts or something? Anyway, I'm waiting for the feeling of something to grab me and shake me up like a test tube full of dust or gay glitter! Ha! Yes, I'm far away from England. Far from home. The cars outside the window are dreaming. The green leafy leaves, huge in approximation, are dawdling around in the September non-wind, bumbling like nice old men, murmuring something like, "Yeeaaahssss." On drugs and dying hard. The fat, suited man sitting directly in front of me looks very formidable. Like a tough-nut to crack. There's something Dick Cheney-ish about him.

Lord knows this life is dull enough without writing and feeling this way. Full of laughter. I suppose I shall have to write another book in DC! Another book! EASY!

Ramadhan 11, DC Metro Train, West Falls Church

Facing Future

Why don't you come close to me
And smile upon my countenance
With white teeth and beaming
Somali-eyes ?
My Friend!

Press your hands onto mine and heartishly talk
Soulenly
        Slavishly
                Give!

If not to me, then some other
Pea-brain.

Ramadhan 28, DC Metro Train, West Falls Church

Where Is the Sun of You?

Where is the sun of you?
The giving child who runs in you?
Who doesn't know or care where to
Doesn't try so hard for why

Where is the bird of you?
The absolute absurd of you?
The squawking joy-box turning view
That slips in waters affirming hue

Where is the dance in you?
The cerulean blueish France in you?
The mountain hiking chance in you
Who does for Dreams, not what is due

      Where are the chains in you?
      The stuffed-up number games in you?
      The fact'ry folded flames in you
      That burn up all the bursted love

Where is the dove in you?
The only living love in you?
The wing'd spirit solitude
That speak to Him like de Lover do

Ramadhan 28, DC Metro Train, West Falls Church

Infinite Future
from the Dupont Circle, North Exit ascension

But what if there were a silent moon,
Growing and receding in our chest-portals to portent the future firmament?

Silent breathing marred moon against
   Black backdrop and
     Breathing beautifully
       Biding and brooding
         In our steel chests of silver silence

Language must be s p a r e and

    not flowery

For you to comprehend the stillness with which this reality so quietly and absolutely lives.

I'm making nothing up. And in case you wondered and now needed proof, let me confirm it for you:
This is not poetry.

There is a moon in your days.

There is a hissing, receding tide when you sleep.
No waves, but a tide, ankle-deep tide
Relentlessly drawing in and falling off

So that you can't tell if it's moved forwards or
Backwards

All as you lay your tender little head on the pillow of this
teasing, testing world.

All because you're a newborn turtle
Trepid-trawling across the beach sand-scape
Silhouetted by the full white moon of *god-god*.

Into your mind comes a rectangle
With spherical elements and foundations,
Rounded all over. Oblong.

All space outside it is, again,
Black:
A swarm of pre-existence.

And all inside the orb of tomorrow is blue belief
Light and deep blue
     A sky
Offering itself in your very first dawn of days

Before language and even purity.

The message feels to be that
This huge planet is your dominion to rule over.
Your spilling Kingdom to uncontain.
The outer version of your very own name.

Ramadhan 29, Dupont Circle, Washington DC

Brief Glimpse / Precarious Future

And look at your reflection!

For how long will you be this young and
Feel this handsome?

Only for today

Perhaps even only for this morning

Tomorrow you'll be someone else
With different motors
Different fuels
Different alternating currents
Different RAM.

.I hope I'm a lion tomorrow.

Of all the people I can be
I like myself most when I'm a lion.

3rd November, DC Metro Train, West Falls Church

Road of I'm Sold / Me Best Friend

I were walking 'long a clean street
Sided with grand old buildings 'round me
Red brick embassies, century histories

When a yellow light breathed d'Sky open

Sun-belief
Everywhere equally

And mine eyes inhaled it
Without looking up
Atoms rushed me
    Smiling face

Ahead me
D'm Flags of Zambia and Iraq
Whistle high with grace in sky

N'Inside there were
Gentle-yellow-laughters
In d'm space between me heart and
Me neck

And as me walked
All 'round there were d'm feeling of
Communion and joking with
God Almighty

Miy Best friend.

09th December, Wyoming Ave, Washington DC

The Face of a Chosen One

Bellasphone. Sophrratis. Conjunctis.

Pearl baby rotates on a disc of wood
Softly around-round
At the speed of a sunny afternoon sleep.

Under him is a juttering civilisation of
Mountain faces
Jagged rock and a billion civilians
None of whom have harp-thoughts or
Journal-chests or
Sunrise-breasts or
Air-eyes.

Just a bunch of hemmed-in statistics.
Newspaper people.
Just a bunch of *bloggers*!
All on the payroll.
Quick in absolute agreement and dispute.

No, this pearl-child is one from one billion.
Won't be peppered or corrupted
Won't be following the fire-fascination
Or drowning away from the bloggers in need.

This boy will hold hands with everyone
Have mirror-eyes
And be loved and ignored equally.

See his young mans hands
Afront a luminous green
With clashing light-blue
Water falling on

Interspersing his fingers
Which make to grasp
As the water touches
Like some eager lover
Opening eyes just before the kiss.

See his wet veins flourish as he
Turns his hands
Revolving them, opened
With glistens of droplets

Kisses and lovelets.

Barack America

Eleven O'Clock, Election Night

I don't give a damn for his never-ending stump speeches
Which I had memorized months ago
And which
Only now I realize
I will never hear again

And I don't give a damn for the polished and well-oiled
Campaign

Or anything else.

Because there is this round
Expansive bulb
Which I keep feeling in my chest
Growing
With a beaming pulse

And although this word has become desensitized to me
In this lingo-politicking year

I know without a doubt
That the smiling orb inside me
Is called hope

4th November, McLean, Virginia

Ballad of Hussein
After John Lennon
After Tony Blair

Don't let me down, don't let me down
Don't let me down, don't let me down

I'm in love for the first time
Don't you know it's gonna last
It's a love that lasts forever
It's a love that has no past

Don't let me down, don't let me down.
Don't let me down, don't let me down.

And from the first time that he really done me,
Ooh he done me, he done me good
I guess nobody ever really done me
Ooh he done me, he done me good

Don't let me down, don't let me down (please)
Don't let me down, don't let me down (please)

January 1969, Twickenham, London

On a Bus
For Arab female student & older lady who were strangers at first

Sun shines in U S A
Born Freedom in Rows that grows
Corn fields by Sky that's wide
Like-hearts that smile and hold

Two ethnicities
Parallax Purpose
Eyes make love
In-this regulated circus

Where's my cynical
Mode of being?
When everyone's Opened
It's all one seeing.

Hold her hand
On the seat of the bus
The sweat glands work
For our communal trust

Hold her hand
Old African-American
Sunglass'd laughs that are
Cool to suffering

14th October, Georgetown, Washington DC

OBAMERICA

What the heaven is going on?

People... Happy?
A nation...... United??
Their better halves ...... SHINING?
Their hope.... Alive and well??
Optimism... Out to play?

I tell you what, if the human race keeps this up, pretty soon people are going to start believing 'it's not the winning but the taking part that counts.'

And if pulses of kindness drop off strangers hearts and
Make the streets a joy-blanket of interwoven gift-hands,

then

Everyone would be flying like Superman and Lois Lane

And Winter would no longer be hard.

8th November, 2nd Ave, NYC

Like God Does It

I want to smile at the kind young Pakistani woman with the black hijab who works here. But each time I look over, she darts her eyes away. Because pretty people do not stare at each other. Must not!

But I don't need or want to stare

Just a second more to be able to smile

.It's so tender.

And the heart I hold inside

Wanting to frisk the ice-world

So sensitively

To touch

To not stain

Leave no trace of my name

To just smooth over
Without worlds tumbling.

7th November, Coney Island, NYC

Afterwords on the text
==

I touched down in a steaming hot, messy and wild New York City just one day before the 4th of July celebrations. I wandered the ridiculously huge streets of the beastly, scary city, completely alone and in cowboy boots that were too hot for an American summer. I was both horrified and excited. So strange it seemed that I was still reading the same novel I had been reading in Brighton, and yet I felt so very far away from the quiet, South-East coast, beach-town life. I began writing the first poems (pages 1-12) at this time. I remember also feeling, as I clumsily explored the streets and parks, that for the first time in my life, I really was without a home. Those first 12 pages would not have existed without this feeling of being a stranger in a new place. It is a scary feeling, and one that I hope everyone reading this has felt, and will feel, as often as is necessary to disrupt the ongoing illusions we buy into as 'adults'.

"Be in this world as a traveler, or a stranger" – the Prophet

The weather was lovely as I sat on a boulder overlooking rowers in their boats in Central Park (the setting for 'Roots' & 'If'). The feeling in-heart was very strange at that moment. *I am alone. This is exciting. I am alone. Where am I going? Why have I come here? I am here. What next?*

There was only so long I could impose upon my uncle in his Queens apartment and so I headed South to be with my family. By August I found myself working as the Media Relations officer for the relatively small-staffed and insanely overworked Embassy of Afghanistan in Embassy Row,

Washington DC. As I alluded to in the afterword of the previous book, suddenly, without warning, I was wearing a suit and tie and walking to work with a briefcase everyday. It was not how I had envisioned my American adventure when I left England.

After the buzz of commuting every day had worn off, as the Autumn came around, I began to feel increasingly sad. It's like that every day, in the hours before the sun sets, and felt increasingly as the sun is setting. Something wants to hold on. Sad to let go of a familiar innocence. That Autumn of the day, alongside the Autumn of the year, tells us, *the ride is over.* As beautiful as it is (and the beauties volume is turned up 100 times on the Autumns of the East Coast in comparison with the UK) one can't help but be aware, even primordially, in ones bones, that darkness lies ahead.

I had no friends, and even for the strangers I met, it was difficult. As someone wise once said in a documentary, it's very difficult to be away from where you grew up because people don't send the same signals. As a writer, it was fun to observe from my distance, and, to be sure, I had already been playing the role of outsider for a long time in my own hometown of Brighton. But when the situation is a reality and not merely an invention for the sake of art, then one is placed in a very different predicament. For the last year or so in England, my ego was able to tell me that I was being an outsider for the sake of my writing. But you are still home. When my weak constitution became too starved, I was always able to call an old friend, or meet a stranger and say "this is MY city, let me show it to you!" (whatever any fool may say, we need people around us, we are social beings). In

America, however, there was no longer a *choice*. I truly was alone.

Without a car, I would often return home from work rather late (this due largely to my own wandering about after work as much late office hours), and without money for a taxi (coupled with a desire to be away from everything) I would spend many hours wandering along the highway –Route 7– until I reached home. I came up with songs and melodies there that I will never ever record, sung for the *now* as it was felt then (which is the same way each of these books have been written). When I made the final turning into my neighbourhood, away from the highway lights, I would look up and see the stars. The large American sky which I had first noticed in 1996 one Summer's evening in Maryland. The large, continent-sized American sky. What was it that made it look so much bigger than England's sky? Isn't the sky the same everywhere? No. I was in a world now. *The other side of the pond*, as we English often call America, is not a pond at all. It is a huge, uncompromising continent. A world. Once or twice, cars sped past and splashed water onto me and my suit. It was very fitting.

What do we do when we suffer? When we hurt? When we feel insecure? We go towards that which is most real to us. Most comforting, yes, but hopefully, if we are intelligent, the most <u>real</u> is the only thing that can truly bring us towards that sense of balance and subjectivity needed in order to see ourselves clearly, know what's going on (and what's going wrong) and enable us to recover enough so that we may fix it. It is a testament to the Islamic life that for most Muslims, both in good times and bad, the most Real thing to us is our faith, and God, almost entirely abstract conceptions (if we must speak from the point of view of the physical world, and we must).

This series of books is about a spiritual journey. An ongoing one, to be sure. Perhaps one reason I have decided to frame the series in this way is that, growing up in England, and now living in the USA, I felt that spirituality was something society not only ignored and underappreciated, but frankly, was almost impossible to access in any real sense. Of course, a bohemian town like Brighton offered one plenty of encounters with New Age wisdoms, but none ever triggered or touched anything of permanence within me. And while a longing for Tradition saw me delve quite extensively into the worlds of Buddhism and Hinduism, I was more drawn to *Tassawuf*, also known as the spiritual science of Sufism. Nevertheless, even this was completely inaccessible outside of books, and one of the first things I learned from Sufi books was that book-knowledge paled in the face of experiential-knowledge. My attraction to this *way* came through its subtlety and understated, sober nature. Starting in the most obvious ways, an adherent may not be easy to visually identify, i.e. he need not wear brightly coloured robes or have to 'look spiritual,' and furthermore, it did not demand from me what my immature and over-thinking mind most liked the sound of, namely a complete detachment/removal from the real world. I was not being asked to go and live in a forest or a desert. And precisely because that is what I often wished to do in times of sadness and exasperation (as well as make myself look different and wear spiritual, strange clothes), I knew I was dealing with something altogether more serious. Not a game, or a hat to try on, which so much of spirituality seemed to me to be. Returning to the idea of retreat- such a disappearing act would be considered far too easy, and if anything, would serve to hinder beginners as much as (if not more than) helping them. Real spirituality for the Sufi begins by hiding what you are doing, and thus not letting anybody know you are even on 'a path,' rather letting your actions be the only thing that speak, all the while fully engaging / negotiating with the world of people, problems and solutions. Given that Sufism is so inextricably bound together with Islam, and given that people's perceptions of Islam are so maligned in the present Western age, perhaps it should be little surprise that Islamic spirituality[2] is so largely unknown.

If it seems as though I am talking only of Western people's perceptions, then it is only partially true. But speaking to that point first, it should be said that there is not much of a mainstream tradition of Westerners having taken a fair, in-depth look at Islamic spirituality, at least not from those who subsequently remained in touch with both 'worlds' afterwards (these worlds are not exclusively East & West, but more, those who have tasted what Sufism is, and those who have not). And this is much needed. When such people are able to act as mediums between these worlds they become blessings, mercies to a population that may otherwise have never studied or uncovered such important wisdoms by themselves. We live in a pop age. Let's not deny it with elitism; we do. An entire generation of Englishmen and Westerners fed off the curiosity of one man who happened to have fame and exposure –George Harrison– and the result is that even to this day, millions of Westerners who have never

---

[2] That is to say *Sufism*

picked up a book on anything related to Hinduism, will have a favorable feeling towards it. What a wonderful thing that is. Some of the younger generation today may not even know who George was, but they're inheritors nonetheless. We're all inheriting from something/s.

The other, far more important reason that the world has misunderstood the concept of spirituality of Islam is that Muslims themselves have not fully understood it. Or, more accurately, they have forgotten it.

> *"Today Sufism is a name without a reality, whereas it once was a reality without a name"* – al Hujwiri

Islam as an organized religion had not been a satisfying thing for me for most of my life. I continued to be loyal to it because I knew it's ideal and its potential were unmatched by anything I had ever read, felt or encountered. And of course, in prayer, all Muslims, indeed all humans, are in a felt agreement. There is something the meditating heart feels, which knows what Truth is. Nevertheless, as far as most outward signs go, Islam had not been what it should have been. Mosques in England were not filled to the brim with smiling faces, or even contented faces, as they undoubtedly should have been. There were some. But it made no sense that they were not *all* like that, and not all *overflowingly* like that. Why was there an air of suspicion in mosques? Why did people judge? Why was intellectuality and more discussion not encouraged? Why did people leave and go home? Where was the community? The **wisdom**? I do not subscribe to the notion that these are typical signs of all religions, as some weary cynics might be thinking at this moment, nodding their heads knowingly as if they know. No. This invasion of Islam was the product of people. Of humans!... Oh, *humans*. You beautiful fools. What can we say about you? Nothing at all, except: *humans are human.*

And humans are the prime reason that Islam (and its inherent spirituality) has not been flourishing as it should, as history has shown that it did in Spain, Eastern Europe, China & the far East etc. It's a story many will have heard before. Put simply, *Saudi* Arabia has, for a long time, controlled what the rest of the world considered 'Real Islam' via it's well-organized and ever-well funded mission to flood the entire world with its pamphlets, imams and ultimately, ideology (Salafi-ism, Wahabi-ism). It is essentially a materialistic ideology, one rooted in mistrust, and very unkind, obtuse obsessions with what constitutes a believer and a non-believer. There was no consideration for verticality in this ideology, no upwards path, just sideways glances, all on the material, worldly level. Such an ideology, which was crafted and refined with power and the elite in mind, was always going to be firmly opposed to the Spiritual Realities that were intended by the Prophet Muhammad as liberation for the masses. And, I must emphasize Liberation, and its meaning in the truest, deepest and most mature sense of the word; no romantic images of Che Guevarra with a rifle (with my apologies and respects to *El Che*), but rather, a silent and invisible awakening at dawn in order to communicate more fully with the Creator and finally subdue, master that which truly weighs us down: our own selves and ego's. A *struggle* for freedom from all that binds us to the ephemeral, to temporality, and a *joyful walking* on paths that take us to things Real, and thus eternal.

Further reading for any on this subject could be beneficial[3]; knowing history enables us to know the present, and I have no desire to recount in detail the atrocious waves of dogmatic ideology that has been pounding (and flooding) our beloved heartland for the last 200-odd years. I find the 1000 plus years that preceded the Salafi-movement to be far more informative and inspiring (so did the Enlightenment).

As I walked to work day after day in the vicious DC Winter, where we suited gerbils burst forth from our commuter trains in mean, me-first sploshes, towards jobs that we could not possibly care passionately about, and as I looked around them all at times, re-remembering that I had been thrust into the middle of a race that I had literally nothing to do with, a question somehow grew in me like a strawberry. A December Strawberry of Mercy. I noticed it one morning, just lingering there in my heart as *pure feeling*. And, for the very first time, I phrased it in my mind. 'Who am I?' is what came out. The sentiment was quickly followed by, 'What am I doing here? What is my purpose?' One can write poetry until his hand falls off (and I was absolutely doing that) but these questions were far larger than even poetry. And I had no answers for them. I walked the streets with no aim. I prayed desperately to a God that I felt so surely, and yet even my religion had become something estranged. In certainty, there was only God (and there might have been a *me*, I was not sure). I suspect that I am not the only one who is able to ignore such soul-stirrings. And indeed, had it not been for the dramatic events that followed soon after (see the next book in the

---

[3] The Salafi Movement Unveiled by Hisham Kabbani; The Wahhabi Mission and Saudi Arabia by David Commins.

series: *The Beautiful / Palace Prayers*) these questions may have disappeared into the folds of the daily grind. Even so, this was the first time such a thought had ever come to me. *Who was I?* Why, I was an *artist!* Surely, the answer was obvious!? But no. No, a thousand times. Human titles do not matter. The heart knows. As they say here in America, *cut the B S!*

In the meantime, through lots of bitterness and unhappiness (the specifics of which I will spare you) I had somehow, during the days and weekends, managed to summon up a beneficent and tender spirit within me. It was as though the more I suffered, the more kind I became, and I wrote pieces like *Life & Heaven, Listening to God..., Pearl* and *Wake up a new man*. If this book did not provide proof, I would not have believed that I could have written such things, given how I felt at the time. And yet as I have noted repeatedly in life: (nearly always after the fact) arts glory lies partly in its ability to down-convert the ugliest of human emotions (or any emotion) into pure energy form. This pure energy is then released in accordance with the direction ones spirit is facing at that moment. You disperse it into infinity, and receive some provision in return for your good act (for if it were not converted, it would have remained active within you and manifested in hurting yourself and/or someone else through less-refined words or actions). Islam and creativity cross-over here, for under the correct guidance, the prayers become inspired and healing, just like art but in a far more penetrating and mystical way. Through the darkest moments, you are aware that He, and no other force, keeps your heart beating, and if you likewise believe in destiny[4], you *know* that

---

[4] One of the six essential Islamic articles of faith

your heart is beating you on to somewhere better. Curiosity for that unknown but better future pushes you forwards. Curiosity keeps the cat alive.

In line with this chord of hope amidst despair, Barack Hussein Obama was elected. He was (and is) a medium between worlds, and everyone knew it even then. I felt bad admitting that I felt hope. I was not taken in by all that corny American nonsense, a part of me said. But I wanted to be. In fact, I longed to be. And so I allowed myself to be. Not because I necessarily believed that everything he said was going to be wonderfully true, but because sometimes in life, your soul has to ride on the back of *something*. If you are stranded in the middle of a desert, you would be a fool not to take a ride from a camel, even if that camel smelled badly. Even if it was a plastic, mechanical camel made in Taiwan. Hope was what they called it. I decided to let myself feel it. Sure enough, the morning after his election victory, there was a genuine sense of peace in the air as I ascended out of the metro station and walked to work. I looked up at the sky. It was a bright morning, even if it was not sunny.

"You are a child of today," said a man who I love. New realities are created and changing continuously and infinitesimally. Words cannot work. Keats knew this well. The finely polished heart is the only thing that can keep up. Beauty must be reflected, and we must not be scared to ride on it, all the way back to its (and *our*) essence.

With apologies and peace,

Yusuf Misdaq,
May 09th 2011, Brooklyn, New York.

The author with his grandfather, the poet Abdul Latif Rashid

Also available & coming soon from Yusuf Misdaq

Lefke Automatic / Destiny of Love (Poetry)	NEFI-BK07
The Beautiful / Palace Prayers (Poetry)	NEFI-BK06
The Butterfly Gate (Poetry)	NEFI-BK04
Into Solidity (Poetry)	NEFI-BK03
Brighton Streets (Poetry)	NEFI-BK02
Pieces of a Paki (Novel)	NEFI-BK01
[No Title] (Documentary)	NEFI-CD03
Maghreb, Isha & Space (LP)	NEFI-CD03
Flowers & Trees (LP)	NEFI-CD02
From a Western Box (LP)	NEFI-CD01

Narayan (Novel)
The Steep Ascent (Novel)

www.ingramcontent.com/pod-product-compliance
Lightning Source LLC
Chambersburg PA
CBHW022122040426
42450CB00006B/805